F

Broth

by Jennifer Marks-Kusturis

illustrations by Scott Angle

Harcourt Brace & Company

Orlando Atlanta Austin Boston San Francisco Chicago Dallas New York Toronto London

Fitch and Gitch
are chums.

Fitch likes to fix lunch.
And Gitch likes to eat
lunch.

3

Fitch fixed a batch
of broth.
Munch, MUNCH!
Crunch, CRUNCH!

"Such a lunch!" said
Gitch. "This broth is
thick and rich! It has
so much froth!"

"It's Froth Broth,"
said Fitch.
"How do you fix it?"
said Gitch.

"Oh," said Fitch, "I put in a pinch of this and a pinch of that. Here, look."

Fitch's Froth Broth

1. Chop up a branch.
2. Put it in a pot with a bunch of rocks.
3. Next, have a bath.
4. Put the bath suds in the pot.
5. Mix the broth.
6. Chill it.
7. Then munch and crunch!